MAGIC OR SCIENCE?

Jean-Christophe Piot

Illustrated by
Zelda Zonk

WS Education

Published by

WS Education, an imprint of
World Scientific Publishing Co. Pte. Ltd.
5 Toh Tuck Link, Singapore 596224
USA office: 27 Warren Street, Suite 401-402, Hackensack, NJ 07601
UK office: 57 Shelton Street, Covent Garden, London WC2H 9HE

National Library Board, Singapore Cataloguing in Publication Data
Names: Piot, Jean-Christophe. | Zonk, Zelda, 1973– illustrator.
Title: Magic or science? / Jean-Christophe Piot ; illustrated by Zelda Zonk.
Description: Singapore : WS Education, [2020] | First published as Magique ou scientifique? by Gulf stream, Nantes (2018).
Identifiers: OCN 1157301038 | ISBN 978-981-122-299-3 (paperback) | 978-981-122-227-6 (hardcover)
Subjects: LCSH: Science--Miscellanea--Juvenile literature. | Magic tricks--Juvenile literature.
Classification: DDC 502--dc23

British Library Cataloguing-in-Publication Data
A catalogue record for this book is available from the British Library.

For any available supplementary material, please visit
https://www.worldscientific.com/worldscibooks/10.1142/11884#t=suppl

Desk Editor: Daniele Lee

Printed in Singapore

CONTENTS

ONE, TWO, THREE, LEVITATE!

Have you ever seen a man sitting a meter high in the air, someone seemingly hovering above the pavement, or a magician whose assistant is suspended above the stage? You must have wondered: What is this mysterious force that defies the most elementary laws of gravity?

If you look closely, all these amazing characters are, in one way or another, connected to the ground: using a cane, an umbrella, a chair, a stick. All you need to do is attach this metal axle to a base on the pavement, and you are all set. If the base is heavy or wide enough, it becomes possible to sit on the small platform at the top without collapsing. A bit like a lamp post! All that's left to do is to keep the charade going to camouflage the whole thing. That's why street performers are always dressed in slightly loose clothes, with long sleeves. Levitation is as simple as a lampstand.

VOTE YOGI!

Meditation is a good way to relax as long as you don't mix things up. In 1992, a famous Indian sage, Maharishi Mahesh Yogi, and his followers entered politics through the Natural Law Party and contested several elections in France. Proclaiming to have yogic flight, a somewhat bizarre version of levitation, they claimed to be able to reduce crime, end wars, and cure diseases, but no one ever saw them flying, only jumping around and sitting in a suit. It was a bit ridiculous and not very effective, resulting in the disbandment of the party in 2001.

REAL LEVITATION, YES, BUT THANKS TO SCIENCE!

Stronger than Master Yoda? Scientists have long since unraveled the mystery of levitation. Using very powerful electromagnets, they used electromagnetic force to hold small objects in the air. Another way is using loudspeakers. Since sound is a wave, all you have to do is find the right frequency to suspend an object in the air between two speakers and it will look like the object is floating on an invisible wave. However, it takes a lot of power to make even a tiny drop of water fly around 160 decibels, that's even louder than a plane taking off!

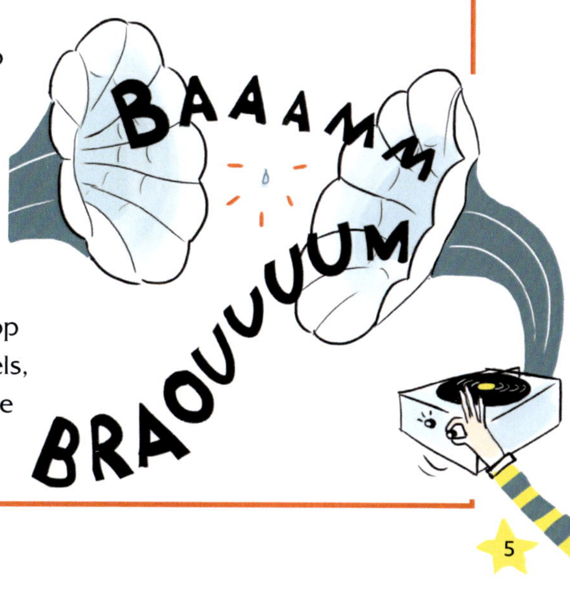

PENDULUM, ASTROLOGY AND OTHER PROPHESIES...

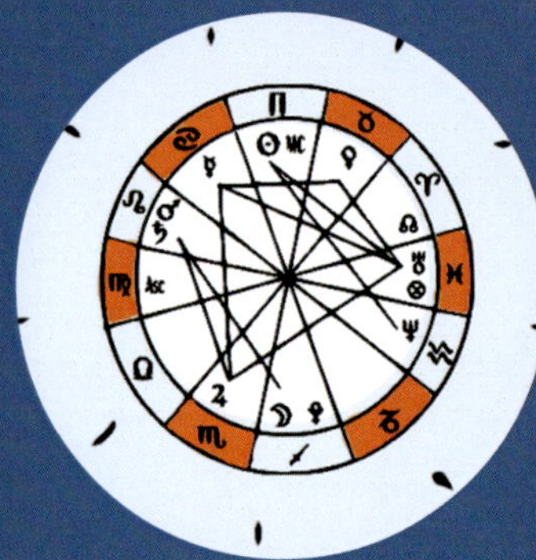

"Always a little further west!"

If you remember Tintin and Professor Tournesol, you know that the latter never separates from his pendulum. With this metal ball suspended on a wire, our favorite scientist is able to find missing objects or solve certain mysteries. Similar to other "radiesthesists," Tournesol also interprets the movements of the sphere when the pendulum hovers over a map or a certain sign.

For people who still believe that it is mysterious magnetic signals that make the pendulum swing, researchers have proved that the pendulum swings simply because the hand of the radiesthesist moves. As calm as he is, with a tiny breath, Professor Tournesol's heart makes the blood in his veins beat. These tiny movements cause the metal sphere he is holding at arm's length to oscillate.

The 13th Zodiac Sign

Capricorn, Leo, or Libra? Your astrological sign corresponds to a constellation, a group of stars hidden behind the Sun at the precise moment of your birth. Since ancient times, astrologers have said that they can describe someone's character and predict their future using the stars. This method is questionable, if only for one reason: they forgot the thirteenth constellation, the Serpentary, located between Scorpio and Sagittarius. This error alone is enough to distort their entire system, conceived around twelve signs and not thirteen. It is better not to rely too much on the stars to know the future.

THE TITANIC PROPHECY

The sinking of the Titanic in 1912 resulted in the deaths of more than 1,500 passengers. A disturbing detail: Fourteen years earlier, a novel had told the story of the Titan, the world's largest ship, sunk by an iceberg on an April night in the North Atlantic. The same name and a similar story where the lifeboats run out! Could the author, Morgan Robertson, have seen the future? However, he certainly knew the sea very well. Icebergs have always been dangerous in the Atlantic in springtime, and shipping companies had been fighting for a long time to build the largest ship in the world. As for the lack of rowboats, it was already a well-known problem. Coincidences, certainly, but no miracle!

READING MINDS? EASY!

You would have already heard of mentalists, magicians who seem to be able to guess very precise things about people chosen from the audience just by looking at them: astrological signs, last holiday destinations, names of their children, professions, etc. without ever making any mistake!

Though gifted, mentalists don't really have magic powers, but rather a good memory, and a strong ability to deduce, without forgetting some tricks done with the help of their accomplices. Often on their television shows, one of their tricks would include, for example, asking an assistant to retrieve the documents that people have to fill out to be allowed to participate in the show. An amazing amount of information is contained there already: name, address, age, place of birth.

Their most effective technique has a funny name: pellet shooting. It's more like hunting, where a hunter shoots a volley of pellets instead of a single bullet, to increase his chances of hitting the target. Instead of saying something like, "Your daddy has heart problems," the mentalist says, "I can see a man in your family has a heart problem, it may be a father, a grandfather, an uncle, a cousin..." Statistically, he is likely to be right: heart disease is very common at a certain age. All he has to do is watch the volunteer's reaction to see if he has nailed it. Clever, isn't he?

CAB FARE

Gary Kurtz is a famous mentalist often invited on TV shows. On one of these shows, he was filmed getting into a taxi just after getting out of the plane, and then talking to the car driver. Unbelievably, the magician guessed a lot of things about this man that he had never seen before! According to Gérard Majax, another magician, the trick is quite simple: an accomplice had simply taken that same taxi to the airport and chatted with the driver before passing on the gathered information to Gary Kurtz. All that remained for the mentalist was to make sure he took the same taxi, which isn't very difficult, especially for a show that wasn't shot live.

CAN YOU SIT ON NAILS OR CHARM A SNAKE?

We often see fakirs in comic books or movies. In India, they are highly respected for their wisdom and meditation skills. However, travellers only tend to recall their most impressive habits, such as spending hours sitting on planks studded with nails! Not only do they not injure themselves, but they even seem to find it quite comfortable.

However, sitting on a nail board does not require any magical power, not even an extra-ordinary resistance to pain. It's a simple matter of weight distribution, just like walking barefoot on sharp rocks. If you stand on one leg, it can get sore very quickly. If you stand normally, it's much easier because two feet support your weight better than one does.

It is the same principle in the case of fakirs: the more nails the board is studded with, the less difficult it is to lean on it. If you sit on 200 nails, each nail will carry your weight divided by 200. If you sit on 400 nails, the load carried by each nail will be divided by 400. On the other hand, no one will ever be able to lean on just one buttock on four or five nails without hurting themselves very badly — even the most gifted fakir, unless he has real magical powers.

SNAKE CHARMERS

If you've ever travelled to the Maghreb or Asia, you may have come across snake charmers. Sitting in their suits, they play the flute in front of a basket from which a cobra or viper emerges. The spectacle is impressive: fascinated, the reptiles wriggle and nod their heads as they watch. Does their master have a gift for controlling these creatures, like Voldemort? No, he doesn't! It's the flapping of the charmer's feet that worries them and makes them stand up out of the basket to watch what's going on. As for the flute, it's not the sound that counts, but its movement. The snake does not dance: it undulates with the musical instrument to control the situation. The art of the charmer is to find the right distance: if he gets too close, the snake will attack; if he stands too far away, the snake may return to its rest...

BREAKING METAL

Imagine this: An illusionist takes a long metal rod on a stage and passes it among the spectators so that everyone can check its solidity. Then he takes this rod and twists it several times using the strength of his hands alone. Amazing! The straight rod is transformed into a real metal knot. Announcing that he will be concentrating to use all the power of his mind, he then places it under a very powerful spotlight, and concentrates very hard. Ta-da! The bar becomes straight again.

This does not need a trick. The bar is certainly made of metal, but of a somewhat special alloy, classified as a "shape memory" material. Though there are many such materials, the most common is a mixture of nickel and titanium with a funny effect: it has the ability to regain its initial shape after bending. If you twist a rod made of this metal and then heat it to the right temperature, it will be as straight as it was at the beginning. On stage, it is the heat of the spotlight that allowed the magician to succeed in his trick. However, these types of alloys are often used in very practical applications, such as eyeglass frames. If you accidentally twist them, all you have to do is to run them under hot water to straighten them back.

MELTING METALS

All metals become soft at a certain temperature. Most metals liquefy above 1000°C, whereas some melt at lower temperatures. For example, mercury, which has long been used in thermometers, becomes liquid above -39°C. Similarly, gallium, though it is very dangerous and should not be played with, can be used in some tricks. This shiny metal melts at exactly 29.8°C. Keep a few shards of it in the fridge before putting them in the palm of your hand and you'll see it liquefy in a minute or two. It has another hidden superpower: if you put it on aluminum, it makes it very brittle. A soda can dipped in gallium will tear like paper!

SPIRIT, ARE YOU THERE? PROBABLY NOT...

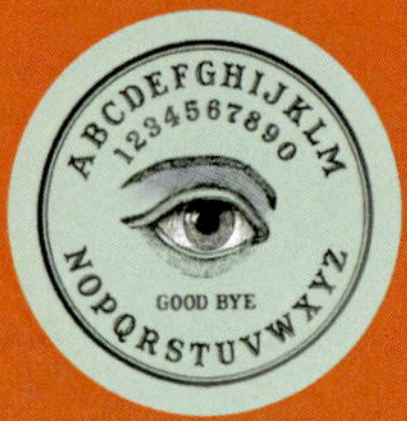

For about two centuries, some people enjoyed ending their evenings with a séance, which refers to a series of methods supposed to allow one to talk to ghosts with the help of a medium capable of interpreting mysterious signs: icy draughts, muffled blows that seem to come from inside the table, stools that start dancing. Scary! Unless you take a closer look.

While some people are truly convinced that they possess extraordinary powers, not all mediums are sincere. We can't count the number of tricks they use to make furniture move at a distance or make strange noises, such as very fine wires, hidden accomplices, and mechanical systems. In a room barely lit by a few candles, anyone can be swayed into believing in the supernatural, especially if you've had a few drinks.

Now let's take a situation where no one cheats. It's late, and some friends have decided to give it a try. Sitting in a circle, they all put a finger on a glass in the middle of the table. Suddenly, the glass moves by itself! Imagine the screams. But scientists have found the explanation, which they call the "ideomotor effect". Even when we think we're not moving, our muscles make lots of small, involuntary movements. Undetectable to the naked eye, these movements are enough to push or move light objects, like a glass on the slippery surface of a well-waxed table.

BOARDS FOR READING THE FUTURE?

Do you know about Ouija boards? We have seen these wooden panels in movies. They have 26 letters of the alphabet, numbers from 0 to 9, and two words: "yes" and "no" painted on them. Some people believe that they allow communication with the afterlife through a droplet-shaped piece of wood. When each participant places their hands on it, it moves to form words. Some mediums even claim that the Ouija board is a very ancient tool, with millenary and mysterious powers. However, this is completely false. These are just toys invented in the United States in 1890, and if the wooden drop moves, it is still because of the ideomotor effect. Ouija boards are as magical as Monopoly boards.

WITCHCRAFT?

Long ago, farmers who wanted to dig a well to provide water to their cattle or fields had to resort to using dowsers to find water. There are still some in use today. These people walked in the fields or meadows holding a small forked branch that looked like the letter Y. At one point, the branch seemed to turn by itself toward the ground, as if it were pointing to a specific place underground. They could find water just by holding a branch!

However, many scientific studies have shown that dowsers have no special powers. In 2001, French researchers experimented by suggesting that some of them go for a walk on a piece of land under which a dozen pipes had been placed. One of these pipes had water circulating in it, and the goal was to see if the candidates could spot it with their wands. None of them managed to do so more than one time out of ten, exactly the same result that anyone would get by chance. However, people may be able to spot the signs that allow them to detect an underground spring, such as a particular type of soil or specific plants on terrains they knew very well.

THE MYSTERY OF FIRE-CUTTERS

For a very long time, in the countryside, when someone got burned with embers or boiling water, "fire-cutters" were called in to treat people instead of doctors. These were the people who were believed to know how to relieve pain and heal burns. Today, the ambulance is the first to be called, but fire-cutters still exist. There are more than 6,000 of them in France. Are they really better? According to the injured, yes. Even doctors admit that their patients actually suffer less. For them, this relief is probably partly due to what is called the placebo effect. If you think that the treatment you receive is effective, it is sometimes enough to feel better, even without any scientific reason. Kind of like the kiss that cures everything for kids. However, to be really honest, no one really understands how it works...

HOW DO YOU WALK ON COALS WITHOUT GETTING BURNED?

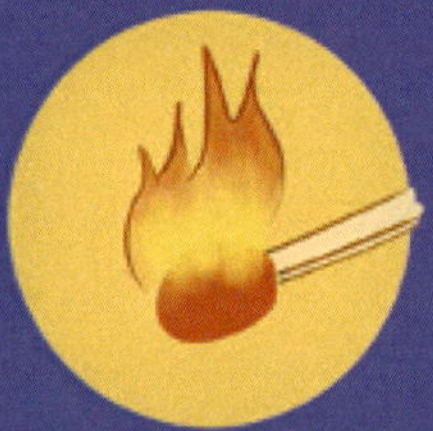

Attention! Hot topic! Do you need supernatural abilities to walk on embers burning at 800°C? Well no. If you don't get hurt, it's for a very simple reason: coal doesn't have time to burn your feet because they stay on the ground for less than half a second with each step. Contrary to what one might think, coal conducts heat much more poorly than other materials, such as metal. It's the same principle as with toasted bread: even if it's hot, you can hold it in your fingers for a few seconds before putting it on a plate. What's more, the skin of your feet is thicker than other parts of your body and it takes longer before you feel a burn. By moving forward calmly, and putting your feet flat to better distribute the heat, you can move forward on embers without hurting yourself.

That said, walking on embers is still very, very dangerous: You only have to stumble or run to get your foot into the hottest parts of the coal bed, the glowing parts. And, anyway, you rarely get out of it without a few blisters.

BREATHE FIRE LIKE A DRAGON

What could be more spectacular than a fire-breather? How is it possible? Does it take a dragon's stomach to project flames of several meters for a few seconds? The explanation is less fantastic. To "spit" fire, spitters fill their mouths with a powder or a liquid like alcohol and spray it all over, like blowing on a pile of flour to form a cloud. When the torch they hold close to their face comes into contact with the powder particles or tiny droplets of liquid, they ignite and form a kind of tongue of fire. Nothing magical, but really risky, if the spitter breathes in too quickly, the flame can come back toward him and hurt him very badly. Not for amateurs!

BEATING THE ODDS

It's hard to find more skilled card players than magicians. What they manage to guess is literally... unbelievable! And yet, one of their secrets is to use fairly simple rules of calculation. How about an example? What do you think are the chances that one of your classmates was born on the same day as you? One in 100 or 300? It's a lot more than that. Mathematicians have calculated that in a class of 25 children, there's a more than 56% chance that two students were born on the same day of the same month.

And this probability increases very quickly: for a group of 35, this "coincidence" has an 81% chance of happening. Even crazier, based on a group of 60 students, the probability is 99%. In other words, it is almost certain that two students in this group would have been born on the same day. These results are of course theoretical, but you can try to prove them, for example, by asking about the birth dates of your schoolmates. It works (almost) every time!

STOPPING TIME

In 1987, a man who called himself a psychic, Uri Geller, was invited to hold a television show. He claimed to be able to stop the watches of remote viewers by the power of his will alone. A few moments later, dozens of people called the show, stunned; their watches had indeed stopped! Unbelievable? Not at all, on the contrary, this requires no "tricks" to succeed, only some knowledge of mathematics. Imagine that 5 million people watch the show with their watch on their wrist. Since a battery works for about 1,000 days, we can calculate that about 5,000 will stop working that day: that's 208 per hour! During the two hours of the show, 516 people will see their watches breakdown at the very moment the "medium" announces it! Uri Geller was counting on this coincidence to impress his audience. You know, you should pay more attention in math class!

HOW DO YOU STICK A KNIFE IN YOUR ARM WITH YOUR FINGERS IN YOUR NOSE?

Imagine: A magician on stage, who has been playing with cards and scarves till now, suddenly pulls a big knife out of his pocket. To show how sharp it is, he slices a fruit with this frightening dagger, and spins it around in the audience before rinsing it in a basin. The next minute, he rolls up his sleeves, and starts lacerating his forearm despite the blood that flows! Even more incredible: a few minutes later, he wipes his arm and shows it to the audience, perfectly intact. Does the magician have the same powers as Wolverine, the superhero whose wounds heal a thousand times faster than ours?

Unfortunately, for him, no. He probably knows more about chemistry than the X-Men character, though. Before the show, he coated his arm with a clear liquid, ferric chloride. Pretending to clean his knife, he then wiped it with a cloth soaked in a second, equally invisible substance, potassium thiocyanate. Okay, these are two products with very complicated names, but they have a remarkable property if mixed together: they form a red liquid that looks a lot like blood... This stuff is often used in movies to simulate wounds. Maybe Wolverine's using it too?

HOW TO EAT A SWORD (WITHOUT SALT OR MUSTARD)

Have you ever seen sword-swallowers? It's impressive, especially when they swallow more than one. In 2015, a German managed to swallow 13 swords at the same time! Do they have superpowers or a steel gullet? Neither, but they know how the human body works very well.

To succeed in their trick, they tip their head back and stand as straight as possible before sliding the blade down their esophagus. To prevent themselves from vomiting, they have learned to control their gullet muscles. When the sword is well coated with saliva or butter (yes!), it goes all the way down to the stomach. And to make this "J" shaped organ a little more vertical and take the shape of an "I", they eat a big meal just before the show! While there is nothing magical about this, it is very, very dangerous as the blade passes just a few millimeters from the heart and lungs.

PHANTOMS, GHOSTS, AND OTHER SPOOKS

In films, television and novels, ghosts have been around since ancient times: Ulysses already encountered them in the Odyssey. In Scotland, they are even used to attract tourists. Those who think they have encountered them say they have seen pale, misty, and almost transparent human forms. Sometimes they describe other phenomena: it gets very cold, objects move, doors creak, etc.

However, scientists have (almost) always found a logical explanation. Noises or bumps in a house, the rush of wind on the tiles, or the chirp of a bird stuck in the chimney, apparitions or visions? An optical illusion is when you think you can see the silhouette of someone in the dark when it is only the shape of a coat rack with a hat on. Next time, when you see an object falling down, check where the cat is first!

As for feelings of sudden discomfort or anxiety, scientists have long known that infrasounds, noises too low for the ear to hear, can make people literally sick! An earthquake, a rash, or even a simple thunderstorm can produce these sounds. If you add fear and lack of sleep to this, you can quickly mistake just about anything for a ghost, especially at night.

THE MAUROUX GHOST

In 2008, Mauroux, a village in the Lot, found itself plunged into a funny story. Several children reported seeing a white silhouette holding a bunch of flowers at night. It happened the following night again in the presence of a friend's mother. The children even filmed the apparition and put it on YouTube, though the video was really blurry. Was there a ghost in Mauroux? Researchers from Grenoble, who came to investigate, soon discovered the truth. The children had made a large cloth doll to prank a friend. The following evenings, one of them disguised himself with a white sheet. When all the adults in the village started to worry, the children didn't dare confess for fear of being punished. Science 1, Ghosts 0!

IMAGES THAT ARE A LITTLE TOO INCREDIBLE...

With good software, nothing is easier than to make up a digital photo, for example, to add a flying saucer to a landscape or a shark behind swimmers. Some fakes are so well done that many people, including specialists, fall for them every day.

Faking is almost as old as photography, an art form born at the beginning of the 19th century. In those days, it was done with plates and then with films. One of the main techniques was double-exposure: by shooting the camera a few times without advancing the film, you could make two images overlap each other. By changing the settings, you could then make one image blurrier and paler than the other. In the 19th century, crooks used this technique to make it look like they had managed to take a picture of a ghost. Dictators like Stalin or Hitler often had old friends erased from official photos because they had turned into troublesome rivals.

Today, advertising is the area where maximum retouching is done to make celebrities slimmer, younger, or more beautiful. This "make-up" is dangerous as by believing that stars have a dream body, we try to reach a perfection that doesn't exist! In order not to be fooled, you can look out for weird details: legs that are too long, skin that looks like plastic, etc.

HELLO NESSIE!

Who doesn't know Nessie, the friendly Loch Ness monster? She became famous in 1934, when a newspaper published a photo taken by a surgeon, Robert Wilson, on the shore of a Scottish lake. Nearly a century later, it is still found everywhere on the Internet, even though it is fake. A few years ago, a friend of the doctor confessed to the deception. He and Wilson tinkered with a model that they welded to the front of a very small pedal-powered submarine, which one of them then piloted below the surface of the lake. Letting only the head and back of their creature emerge, all that remained was to take the picture at the right time and against the light to obtain a deceptive silhouette. Even today, tourists continue to scan the surface of the lake with their smartphones in hand. One never knows...

BERMUDA SHORTS: A TRIANGLE THAT DOESN'T GO AROUND IN CIRCLES

In 1945, five planes disappeared off the American coast during a training mission, "Flight 19". This story caught the attention of journalists on another part of the Atlantic Ocean that connects Florida, Puerto Rico, and the Bermuda Islands. The Bermuda Triangle quickly became famous for a series of mysterious cases: murderous shipwrecks, unexplained disappearances, strange breakdowns. The myth of the Bermuda Triangle was born and was nourished by hundreds of books and films that multiply more or less serious explanations. Some talk about secret military experiments, or attribute the cases to aliens! However, here again, nothing supernatural: if so many ships and planes disappeared there, it was simply because air and sea traffic is very frequent in this immense area (seven times the size of France) and known for its difficult weather: thunderstorms, tornadoes, fogs. If we look at accident statistics, the Bermuda triangle is no more dangerous than other areas. Moreover, no company asks its ships or planes to go around it.

THE BLOOP: A CRY IN THE OCEAN

In 1997, an American oceanographer captured a strange sound off the coast of South America. Extremely loud, it sounded something like "bloop"! It was very powerful and could be heard within a radius of 5,000 kilometers! An unknown underwater civilization? Unlikely. An animal? It would have to be a hundred times bigger than the biggest whale. In fact, researchers think that the bloop is probably due to an "ice quake", a phenomenon that occurs when a huge iceberg breaks off.

FAKE GHOSTS AND REAL WRECKS

There are many tales of ghost ships such as the story of the Flying Dutchman, a cursed sailing ship condemned to roam the oceans with its crew of skeletons. Like in *Pirates of the Caribbean*!
In fact, most of these stories were probably invented by sailors, who must have had a lot of fun coming up with them. The reality, however, are the floating wrecks and boats abandoned because of a storm or a fire, which continue to drift away. Not only is it impressive, but it's dangerous. When the risk of accident is too great, we send out warships to complete the sinking.

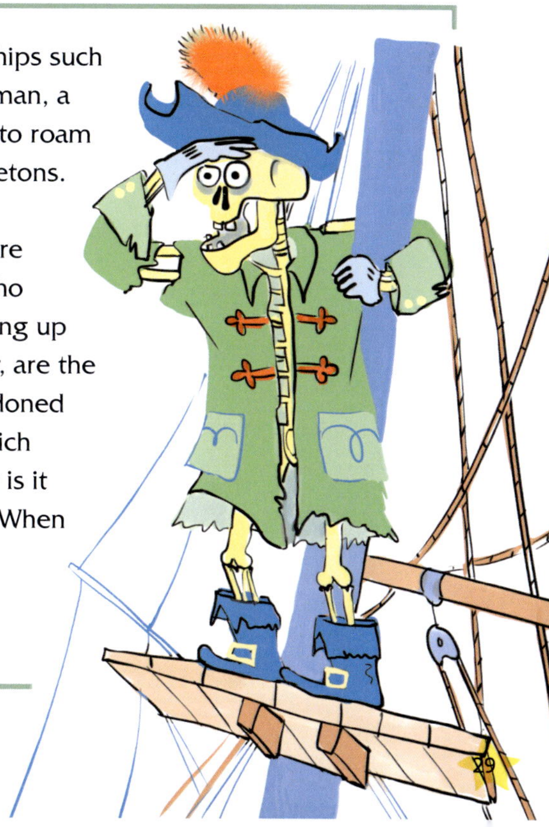

CIRCLES IN WHEAT FIELDS

In 1978, a curious phenomenon appeared in England. Flattened ears of wheat suddenly formed large circles in the middle of the fields. When viewed from the sky, it was impressive! In the following years, these shapes appear all around the world and became more and more complex. Of course, UFO enthusiasts were quickly convinced of one thing: the crop circles are messages left by extraterrestrial visitors.

The explanation is much more mundane. The first crop circle came out of the imagination of two English farmers pranksters. To trace them, they simply used a plank. By attaching it to a rope tied to a stake planted in the ground, they flattened the ears of corn to form almost perfect circles... And to avoid leaving traces of their passage by breaking stems, they moved on some sort of stilts up to the center of the fields.

Since then, many budding artists have developed their own techniques. Today, they even use GPS and microwave machines, capable of flattening a large number of stems at high speed! All this allows them to create increasingly impressive and precise advertisements or works of art. It's still not magic, but it's a good example of English humor.

IN SEARCH OF ALIENS

Searching for signs of an alien civilization from your home? It's possible, thanks to SETI, a very sophisticated American astronomy program that tries to locate the signals of another life in the universe, but requires countless calculations and demands a lot of computer power. To solve the problem, the University of Berkeley in California, had the idea of asking Internet users around the world to "lend" some of their machines by installing the SETI@Home software. SETI@ Home software allows wave analysis to be spread over hundreds of thousands of computers connected to the Internet, instead of being computed by a single computer. Since 1999, four million people have downloaded the software. If we ever find an extraterrestrial message, it might be with their help, why not with your help as well?

WHEN THE OLDEST MAN IN THE WORLD WAS A FAKE

At the end of the 19th century, there was a great deal of interest in skeletal fossils found in certain rocks. Since it doesn't take more than a small hammer, brush, and magnifying glass to get started, many researchers became interested.

In 1899, an English lawyer, Charles Dawson, ran into workers digging along a road in Piltdown. Upon closer inspection of their hole, he discovered a human jaw and skull, surrounded by a few reddish animal fossils. Very excited, he called two learned friends, Woodward and Teilhard de Chardin. After 13 years of work, came the announcement: they had unearthed the oldest Englishman in the world: 500,000 years old. For years, they thought they had found what they called the "missing link," a humanoid intermediate between monkey and man. Even if some specialists doubted it, no one dared to say that this man from Piltdown seems a little strange.

We had to wait 40 years for other scientists to prove that the skull was only 600 years old, that its jaw belonged to an orangutan and that its teeth had been filed! Finally, we realised that all these bones have been chemically stained to age them. Not only is the man from Piltdown fake, but he had been carefully made! It remains to be seen who could have pulled off such a hoax. We'll probably never know, but to fool so many experts, it's likely that the culprit was a scientist.

HOLY GALILEO!

Sometimes scientists can come to terms with the truth even without experimenting. You may have heard of Galileo, a 17th century Italian scientist who proved that the Earth revolved around the sun. Galileo is also famous for establishing one of the bases of the scientific methods: you have to experiment with a theory to prove it. The problem is that Galileo himself tended to forget his own advice. No scientist today has been able to reproduce the results of his experiments on falling objects, and for good reason: it is impossible anywhere but in a vacuum. However, Galileo was sure of himself and his observations to make his theory known without going through a formal experiment.

GO TO SLEEP!

Have you ever had that feeling that your mind is somewhere else while you're doing something, for example in class, when you're sitting down but your mind slips away? Hypnosis looks like that, except that it's a condition induced by a specialist instead of just happening by chance. Unfortunately, it tends to have a bad reputation: the fault lies with magicians who pretend to put people to sleep at will to force them to do what they want.

However, hypnosis is not magic, and its effects are very real. Since scientists now have machines that can examine the brain's functioning in real-time, it's even been proven that some areas "sleep" while others are activated. In fact, it has been used in medicine for almost 100 years, to help people sleep better, to help them quit smoking or simply to make them feel more relaxed. This is a far cry from show hypnosis!

HYPNOTIC SURGERY

If you have been put to sleep for an operation such as appendicitis, you know that waking up is not necessarily very pleasant: you may have a headache, feel like throwing up, etc. To avoid these very difficult moments, more and more hospitals are offering patients the choice to undergo surgery under hypnosis. Everything happens as in a normal operation, but the anesthetist does not completely sedate the patient. He simply gives them a sedative before hypnotizing them, so that they do not feel any pain during the operation. It's like at the dentist's: when he puts a tooth to sleep, you can feel that he is treating a cavity, but it doesn't hurt. Of course, the anesthetist is always there to put the person completely to sleep during surgery if he or she so wishes.

WHEN THE AUTO-MATION'S TOO GOOD TO BE TRUE...

Long before the invention of robots, man devised mechanisms capable of mimicking movement, sometimes very sophisticated. For example, Charlemagne received a beautiful hydraulic clock as a gift from Sultan Haroun al-Rashid. Thanks to a host of pipes and tiny fittings, every noon a small door opened to let out twelve miniature sculptures of horsemen. Sometimes these automatons were so extraordinary that they were seen as a form of magic. Some inventors were even accused of having made a deal with the devil to create cursed machines capable of imitating life.

In 1770, one of them began to circulate around the major cities of Europe. It was called the Mechanical Turk, an automaton dressed in a cape and turban, sitting behind a chessboard on a large desk. Not only was the famous Turk able to move pawns, madmen, and knights, but he also seemed to think. Otherwise, how else could he be able to adapt to the moves of his human opponents? And even better, to beat the best players of his time?

Soon, the whole of Europe was wondering if the mechanics were enchanted. Obviously, there's something in the Turk. The gears shown to the spectators before each session to prove that there was no trickery were a decoy. Behind the gears, there's a tiny room left for a little accomplice. As each piece was equipped with a magnet, every movement played on the board, on the surface, moved a replica underneath, allowing the hidden player to follow the game. Thanks to a system of levers and strings, he could manipulate the Turk, who turned, opened his hand and closed it on this or that piece to make it slide.

A VERY HUMAN HUMANOID

In 1905, Enigmarelle, a strange humanoid the size of a human being, with a painted face and long hair toured the theatres of Europe and the United States. To prove to the public that there was no trickery, its inventor dismantled his legs before each show. However, Enigmarelle still achieved incredible things: once he was back on his feet, he walked, rode his bike, and even managed to write his name with chalk on a blackboard. Again, nothing supernatural though. There was indeed an operator inside the machine, simply chosen because he had no legs, who operated a series of mechanisms and controls connected to small electric motors.

ARCHAEOLOGICAL MYSTERIES

By digging everywhere, archaeologists found very, very surprising things. In Costa Rica, they discovered hundreds of perfectly round stone balls. Some measure a few centimeters in diameter, but the largest is more than two meters high and weighs 16 tons. I promise, it wasn't aliens who had fun transporting them there, but people who have now disappeared, called the Diquis. They collected stones already rounded by erosion in the bed of a torrent and cut them before polishing them with sand.

Impressive? Maybe not as much as the underwater ruins on Yonaguni Island, near Japan. In 1985, a diver discovered a large stone structure 75 meters long. Up close, it looks like a series of stairs, several meters high and very regular. A sunken temple? An ancient bridge, flooded after a tsunami? It's hard to say: 30 years after this discovery, scientists still don't know whether Yonaguni's structure is natural or man-made. A real mystery.

STRANGE SKULLS

The impressive "crystal skulls," discovered in South America in 1924, have long remained a mystery. For decades, it was believed that these famous quartz sculptures were made by the Aztecs or Mayans. But, since it was not understood how, some people claimed that the skulls were made by aliens. Others began to say that there were twelve skulls, and that the one who gathered them all would be rewarded with fantastic powers! The solution is less fantastic: thanks to recent techniques, scientists have proved that crystal skulls were neither ancient nor magical, but were made with the help of modern machines. They are fakes, and it must be admitted that they are a bit creepy...

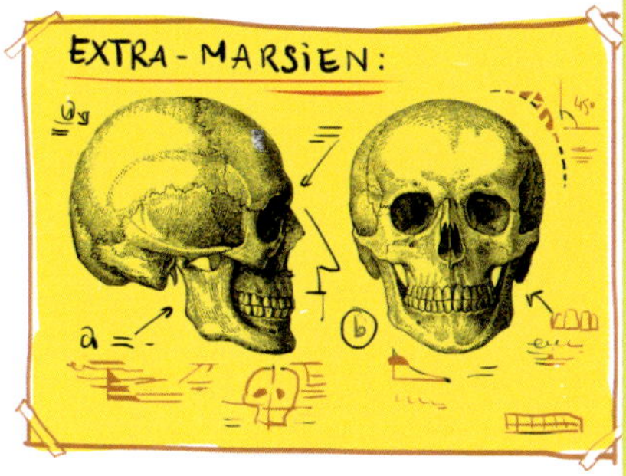

GOLD MAKERS

Mastering matter, finding the secret of eternal life, becoming invisible! Since ancient times, many scientists have practiced alchemy, most often in the secrecy of their laboratories. They are the ancestors of today's chemists who discovered sulfuric acid, antimony, and phosphorus. In the Middle Ages, famous alchemists such as Albert the Great, Nicolas Flamel, or Paracelsus even believed they could discover the secret of the Philosopher's Stone, a strange stone capable of changing a metal like lead into gold, but no one ever succeeded.

However, modern scientists are quite capable of turning lead into gold. It must be said that they work with equipment more powerful than a cauldron and a few stills. What they do know is that atoms have a nucleus made up of protons and neutrons. By comparing a gold atom and a lead atom, they realised that the latter has three protons and eight neutrons more than a gold atom. To turn lead into gold, they just have to tear them out! You can do that using a particle accelerator, a machine capable of throwing atoms against a wall at a very high speed. As they pass through, a very small part of the lead atoms lose their particles and turn into gold atoms.

The problem is that it would take years to get a few grams of gold and it costs several thousand euros per hour to operate a particle accelerator. In other words, we know how to make gold, but it costs much more than it yields. Nevertheless, it would be enough to make medieval alchemists jealous.

THE DANGEROUS GAMBLE OF THE SWINDLERS

The desire to make gold soon gave ideas to a few crooks who saw it as a good way to swindle the naïve. And each to their own formula! The most convincing ones pretended to mix molten metals in a crucible using a long stick. In front of their stunned customers, the mixture suddenly took on a golden color. Their trick? The wand was hollow, closed with a wax pad and filled with gold powder. As it melted, the stopper allowed it to flow out and mix with the metal, but this little game was risky. In 1637, a certain Dubois managed to deceive Louis XIII and Richelieu for several weeks, before getting caught. He ended up hanged.

STRANGE CONSTRUCTIONS

The pyramids of Egypt, the menhirs of Carnac, the dolmens of Stonehenge. Looking at such constructions, it is impossible not to ask the question: how did the ancients manage to build such monuments without our modern machines? Many people are ready to believe in far-fetched explanations: involvement of the gods, help from extraterrestrials, magical rituals. Archaeologists have shown that it was possible with the techniques of the time and a lot of work.

For a long time, the 887 moaï of Easter Island remained a mystery. No one understood how its inhabitants managed to erect these huge stone statues. The largest weighs 80 tons (the weight of a locomotive), and they were sometimes transported over 10 kilometers. In 1998, a team of archaeologists developed a technique that allowed them to move a 12-ton statue! To do this, they laid it on a kind of sled, which they then slid over logs. Working 5 hours a day, they managed to cover 15 kilometers in less than a week. In 2011, other archaeologists managed to straighten a 10-ton moaï and moved it forward in a vertical position using simple ropes. Exactly as in an old story of the island, which tells that once sculpted, the moaï walked to their location along the coast.

THE WORLD'S OLDEST MYSTERY?

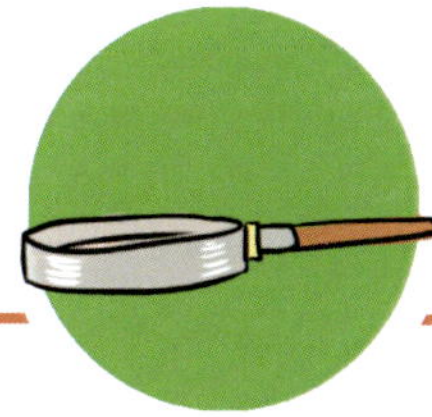

Looking for the oldest temple in the world? Head for Turkey! 14,000 years ago, the inhabitants of Göbekli Tepe built one of the first stone buildings of mankind here. On top of a hill, archaeologists found strangely carved monuments, which they first thought were tombs. They were not tombstones, but the tops of pillars five or six meters high, forming wide circles. Skillful sculptors had carved beautiful wild animals into them: snakes, ducks, bulls, scorpions and even some ants. All this happened 75 centuries before the pyramid of Keops. But the real mystery lies elsewhere: the hill is not natural, but man-made. In other words, 8,000 years ago, the people who lived in Göbekli Tepe suddenly decided to bury the building and no one knows why yet...